The World of Bamboo

By Margaret Williamson

Discover Plants and Animals
Vowel Teams in Two Syllable Words

T0062069

Scan this code to access the Teacher's Notes for this series or visit
www.norwoodhousepress.com/decodables

NORWOOD HOUSE PRESS

DEAR CAREGIVER, *The Decodables* series contains books following a systematic, cumulative phonics scope and sequence aligned with the science of reading. Each book allows its reader to apply their phonics knowledge in engaging and relatable texts. The words within each text have been carefully selected to ensure that readers can rely on their decoding skills as they encounter new or unfamiliar words. They also include high frequency words appropriate for the target skill level of the reader.

When reading these books with your child, encourage them to sound out words that are unfamiliar by attending to the target letter(s) and sounds. If the unknown word is an irregularly spelled high frequency word or a word containing a pattern that has yet to be taught (challenge words) you may encourage your child to attend to the known parts of the word and provide the pronunciation of the unknown part(s). Rereading the texts multiple times will allow your child the opportunity to build their reading fluency, a skill necessary for proficient comprehension.

You can be confident you are providing your child with opportunities to build their decoding abilities which will encourage their independence as they become lifelong readers.

Happy Reading!

Emily Nudds, M.S. Ed Literacy
Literacy Consultant

Norwood House Press • www.norwoodhousepress.com
The Decodables ©2024 by Norwood House Press. All Rights Reserved.
Printed in the United States of America.
367N–082023

Library of Congress Cataloging-in-Publication Data has been filed and is available at
https://lccn.loc.gov/2023010425

Literacy Consultant: Emily Nudds, M.S.Ed Literacy
Editorial and Production Development and Management: Focus Strategic Communications Inc.
Editors: Christine Gaba, Christi Davis-Martell
Photo Credits: Shutterstock: 2p2play (p. 16), adul24 (p. 12), Almira Elmida Kustari (p. 20), ANEK SANGKAMANEE (pp. 6–7), Anton Watman (p. 19), asharkyu (p. 18), Asia Images (p. 17), Dej Mann (p. 11), Dewi Okky Rostiani (p. 5), Diane N. Ennis (p. 5), Eugen Haag (p. 19), Hvoya (p. 9), Irina Adamovich (p. 5), Katacarix (cover, p. 8), K REEM STUDIO (p. 14), Macrovector (covers), MG photos (p. 19), NavinTar (p. 21), Orawan Jaturasitha (p. 21), Pakhnyushchy (p. 15), Patryk Kosmider (p. 4), sarayuth3390 (p. 10), ThiPhao (p. 13), VictorN (p. 20), vivatchai (p. 20).

Hardcover ISBN: 978-1-68450-685-9   Paperback ISBN: 978-1-68404-905-9
eBook ISBN: 978-1-68404-960-8

Contents

What Is Bamboo?

Bamboo is giant grass that looks like a tree. It is the fastest growing plant on Earth. It has shallow roots or **rhizomes**. The rhizomes grow shoots. These shoots grow into hard woody poles called **culms**.

Bamboo grows in a clump or colony. It is the only type of grass that can grow into a forest. New shoots continue to sprout from the culms. The growth repeats until it is time for the bamboo to flower.

This is a bamboo forest in Japan.

Little bamboo plants are often green.

You can see blue bamboo in California.

There are many kinds of bamboo. It is found all over the world. It comes in different shapes, sizes, and colors.

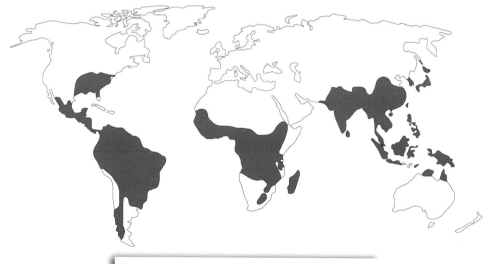

The purple in this map shows where you can find bamboo forests.

5

How Does Bamboo Grow?

Like grass, bamboo grows quickly. The rhizomes creep beneath the ground. They send up new shoots along the way. This means bamboo will come back without having to be replanted.

FUN FACT

Not all bamboo plants are the same. There are about 1500 different kinds of bamboo.

Young bamboo shoots pop up.

Bamboo culms can grow three feet in a day. Each section of the culm contains a **node**. The node strengthens the pole. It takes about three months for the culm to finish growing. Then branches begin to grow from the nodes. Leaves start to appear.

Bamboo culms must finish growing before any leaves appear.

Bamboo farmers plant and grow bamboo.

It takes about five years for the **tissue** in the bamboo to harden. Then it is ready to harvest.

The Bamboo Harvest

Bamboo is harvested during the dry season. It is cut before sunrise. The culms have too much sap in the daytime. If there is too much sap, the bamboo won't dry.

A farmer cuts a shoot of bamboo.

Bamboo culms with lots of sap are very heavy to carry. After cutting, the bamboo is left to dry. It must be done slowly. This prevents cracking. It stops insects from getting inside the plant.

Dry bamboo can be chopped up to make **fiber**.

The Bamboo Flower

A bamboo plant blooms only once in its lifetime. The flower contains lots and lots of seeds. Once the seeds are released, the plant dies. When a bamboo forest dies, it takes about 20 years before a new forest grows.

Bamboo has small flowers.

Here is a bamboo forest in Japan.

When a bamboo forest dies, it hurts the community. There is no **timber**. People lose jobs. Animals lose their homes. Some animals become **endangered**.

It is sad to see bamboo die.

Rats come and feed on the bamboo seeds. Rats can be harmful to the community. They can make people and other animals sick.

Rats feed at night because they are nocturnal animals.

Bamboo Benefits

Bamboo helps the environment. It can grow fast. It collects more **carbon dioxide (CO_2)** than other plants. It releases more **oxygen (O_2)** into the air. It keeps the air cool.

Bamboo keeps the air clean and fresh.

We need the fresh oxygen that plants make.

Bamboo roots hold soil in place. Even **monsoon** winds can't blow the poles down.

Bamboo plants have many strong roots.

Many birds, animals, and insects live in a bamboo forest. It provides them with food. It keeps them safe.

Giant pandas mostly eat the shoots, poles, and leaves of the bamboo plant. They only eat a tiny bit of other foods.

Bale monkeys eat bamboo leaves and shoots.

Gorillas eat bamboo too.

Adult pandas eat 25 to 85 pounds of bamboo each day.

Red pandas eat bamboo, but they also eat bugs and leaves.

Gorillas eat many kinds of plants but bamboo is a favorite food.

Bamboo lemurs live in bamboo forests.

19

Bamboo Products

Bamboo has great value.

Large poles are used in buildings. Thin poles are used to weave furniture. Bamboo fiber is spun into clothing. Bamboo lumber can be cut and pressed into floorboards. It can even be used to make skateboards and fishing rods.

Bamboo can make a bridge.

This house is made from bamboo.

A man is punching holes in the bamboo to make furniture.

Bamboo is used when cooking.

Sushi rolling mats can be made from bamboo.

Bamboo baskets can be used to make yummy food.

Many people agree. Bamboo is indeed a useful plant. It grows fast. It is strong and **renewable**. People can make things with bamboo. Bamboo helps many animals and people everyday.

The first firecrackers were made with bamboo. A bamboo cannon makes a very loud bang.

Glossary

carbon dioxide (CO_2) (kar-bĭn dī-ŏk-sīd**):** an invisible gas that is in the air; used by plants during photosynthesis

culms: the hollow stems of grass

endangered (ĕn-dān-jərd): an animal or plant in danger of dying off

fiber (fī-bər): a thread of plant tissue

monsoon: weather that brings high winds and rain

node: a swelling or knot in a stem

oxygen (O_2) (ŏk-sĭ-jən**):** an invisible gas that is in the air; people must breathe it in to live

renewable (rē-noo-ə-bəl): a resource that can't be used up

rhizomes (rī-zōmz): long roots below the ground that produce shoots above the ground

timber: wooden beam or board

tissue: a group of cells in a plant; holds cells together

Index

Two Syllable Vowel Teams

agree	contains	monsoon	shallow	value
appear	floorboards	released	skateboards	without
bamboo	indeed	repeats	tissue	woody
beneath	monkeys	season		

High-Frequency Words

after	different	kinds	live	over
air	even	large	new	very
also	found	little	only	world
animals	great			

Challenging Words

buildings	community	flower	harden	ready
California	environment	furniture	heavy	releases
colony	floorboards	giant		